CHASE

© 2014 Spin Master. All Rights Reserved.

© 2014 Spin Master. All Rights Reserved.

SKYE

© 2014 Spin Master. All Rights Reserved.

© 2014 Spin Master. All Rights Reserved.

© 2014 Spin Master. All Rights Reserved.

RUBBLE

© 2014 Spin Master. All Rights Reserved.

HOW MANY WORDS

How many words can you make using the letters in:

ALL PAWS ON DECK

_____

_____

_____

_____   _____

_____   _____

_____   _____

_____   _____

_____   _____

_____   _____

_____   _____

© 2014 Spin Master. All Rights Reserved.

ALL PAWS ON DECK

© 2014 Spin Master. All Rights Reserved.

© 2014 Spin Master. All Rights Reserved.

The PAW Patrol is on the job.

© 2014 Spin Master. All Rights Reserved.

Ready to dive in!

© 2014 Spin Master. All Rights Reserved.

Rubble on the double!

© 2014 Spin Master. All Rights Reserved.

Ruff-ruff rescue!

© 2014 Spin Master. All Rights Reserved.

Skye is ready to fly.

© 2014 Spin Master. All Rights Reserved.

Green means go!

© 2014 Spin Master. All Rights Reserved.

PAW Patrol, ready for action, Ryder!

© 2014 Spin Master. All Rights Reserved.

BADGE MATCH

Match each badge to the right PAW Patrol pup.

1 ___

2 ___

3 ___

4 ___

5 ___

6 ___

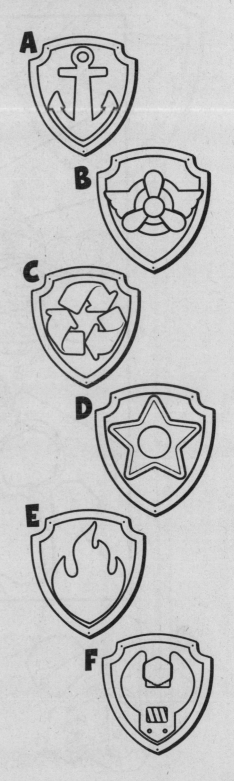

A

B

C

D

E

F

Answer: 1.D, 2.F, 3.A, 4.E, 5.C, 6.B

© 2014 Spin Master. All Rights Reserved.

MISSING PIECE

Which paw print completes the picture?

A

B

C

© 2014 Spin Master. All Rights Reserved.

Answer: C

PUPS AWAY!

© 2014 Spin Master. All Rights Reserved.

Rocky to the rescue!

© 2014 Spin Master. All Rights Reserved.

WHICH IS DIFFERENT?

Which Rocky is different from the others?

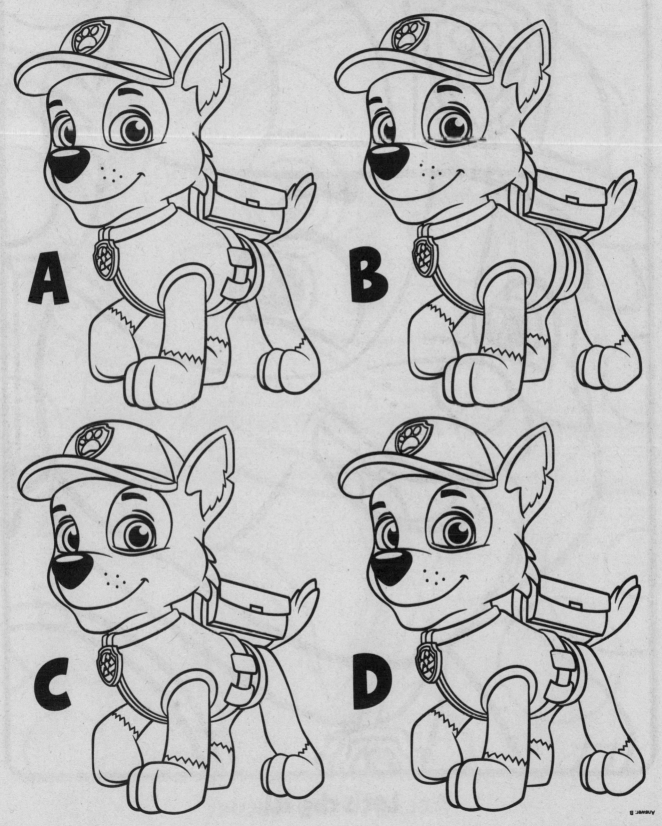

A

B

C

D

© 2014 Spin Master. All Rights Reserved.

Answer: B

Let's dig it!

© 2014 Spin Master. All Rights Reserved.

SHADOW MATCH

Which shadow matches Rubble?

A

B

C

Answer: A

© 2014 Spin Master. All Rights Reserved.

No job is too big.

© 2014 Spin Master. All Rights Reserved.

No pup is too small!

© 2014 Spin Master. All Rights Reserved.

These paws uphold the laws.

© 2014 Spin Master. All Rights Reserved.

LET'S DRAW!

Use the grid to draw Chase.

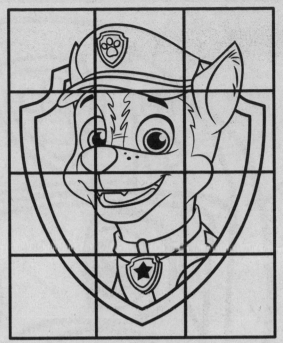

© 2014 Spin Master. All Rights Reserved.

© 2014 Spin Master. All Rights Reserved.

WHICH PATH?

Which path leads Ryder to Zuma?

A

B

C

© 2014 Spin Master. All Rights Reserved.

© 2014 Spin Master. All Rights Reserved.

© 2014 Spin Master. All Rights Reserved.

WORD SEARCH

Look up, down, and across for these words.

PUPPY   BALL   RESCUE
BONE   PLAY   PAW
YELP   HOWL   PATROL

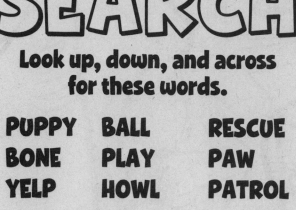

C E Q G V A P L A Y
O B L M P R O W P D
V P C B A L L F B P
L U Y S W N T E R A
F P A H O W L G S T
D P C M L T E Y M R
G Y R E S C U E H C
E W N L G I P L S L
L T B O N E B P X D
Y M O Z P R A Q W E

© 2014 Spin Master. All Rights Reserved.

© 2014 Spin Master. All Rights Reserved.

© 2014 Spin Master. All Rights Reserved.

LET'S DRAW!

Use the grid to draw Marshall.

© 2014 Spin Master. All Rights Reserved.

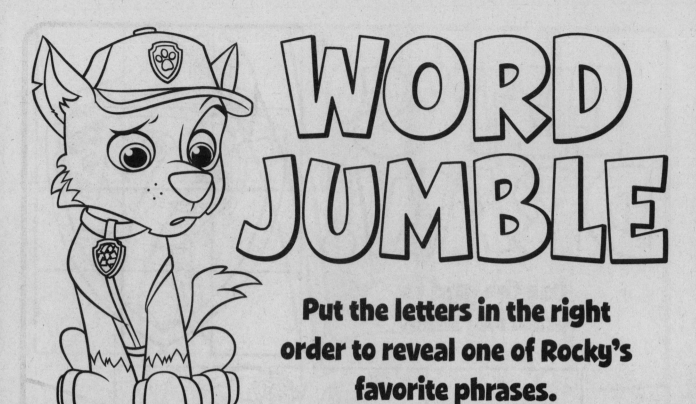

WORD JUMBLE

Put the letters in the right order to reveal one of Rocky's favorite phrases.

NODT ELSO TI ,

_ _ _ _ _ _ _ _ _ _

SEERU TI !

_ _ _ _ _ _ _ _ _!

© 2014 Spin Master. All Rights Reserved.

Answer: DON'T LOSE IT - REUSE IT!

© 2014 Spin Master. All Rights Reserved.

HOW MANY WORDS

How many words can you make using the letters in:

JUST YELP FOR HELP

_____

_____

_____

_____

_____

_____

_____

_____

_____

_____

_____

_____

_____

_____

_____

_____

_____

_____

_____

© 2014 Spin Master. All Rights Reserved.

PAW Patrol is on a roll!

© 2014 Spin Master. All Rights Reserved.

© 2014 Spin Master. All Rights Reserved.

A-MAZE-ING!

Help Marshall find the fire.

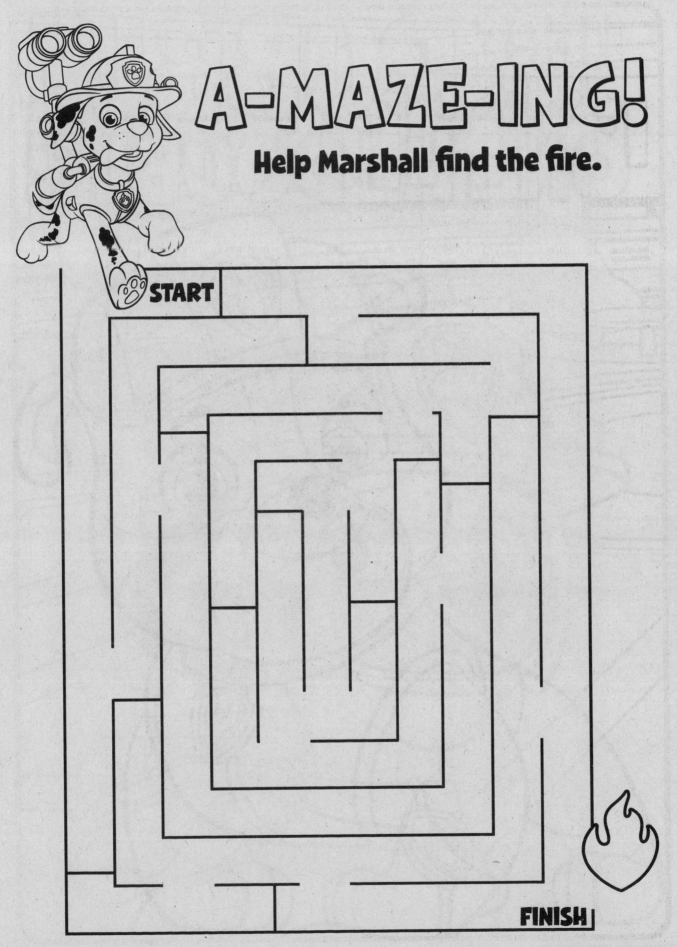

START

FINISH

© 2014 Spin Master. All Rights Reserved.

HERE COMES RUBBLE ON THE DOUBLE!

© 2014 Spin Master. All Rights Reserved.

MARSHALL

ZUMA

© 2014 Spin Master. All Rights Reserved.

My
nose
knows!

© 2014 Spin Master. All Rights Reserved.

© 2014 Spin Master. All Rights Reserved.

CHASE is on the CASE!

© 2014 Spin Master. All Rights Reserved.

ROCKY

CHASE

© 2014 Spin Master. All Rights Reserved.

WORD SEARCH

Look up, down, and across for these words.

SKYE   RUBBLE   PUP PACK
CHASE   ZUMA   PAW PATROL
ROCKY   RYDER   MARSHALL

```
R A B Q V C H A S E
Y O P R U B B L E W
D S M D H X L T R Z
E P A W P A T R O L
R O R C U D B O L M
S M S B P E Q C D R
C E H F P H S K Y E
B R A S A G L Y F A
O G L W C F N P Z Q
M Z L E K Z U M A R
```

© 2014 Spin Master. All Rights Reserved.

THIS PUP'S GOTTA FLY!

© 2014 Spin Master. All Rights Reserved.

Let's Play!

© 2014 Spin Master. All Rights Reserved.

I CAN DIG IT!

© 2014 Spin Master. All Rights Reserved.

© 2014 Spin Master. All Rights Reserved.

WORD SEARCH
Zuma wants to play!

Look up, down, and across for these words:

BONE	TOYS	BALL
CHEW	PLAY	PULL
DIG	RUN	CATCH

P C A T C H E T
A H G O P K D X
V E O Y F M I B
M W N S H V G Z
P Q L B O N E A
U S C A J I P R
L B P L A Y L U
L E S L O Q S N

© 2014 Spin Master. All Rights Reserved.

Pups at Play

© 2014 Spin Master. All Rights Reserved.

© 2014 Spin Master. All Rights Reserved.

A-MAZE-ING!

Help Rocky find the bone.

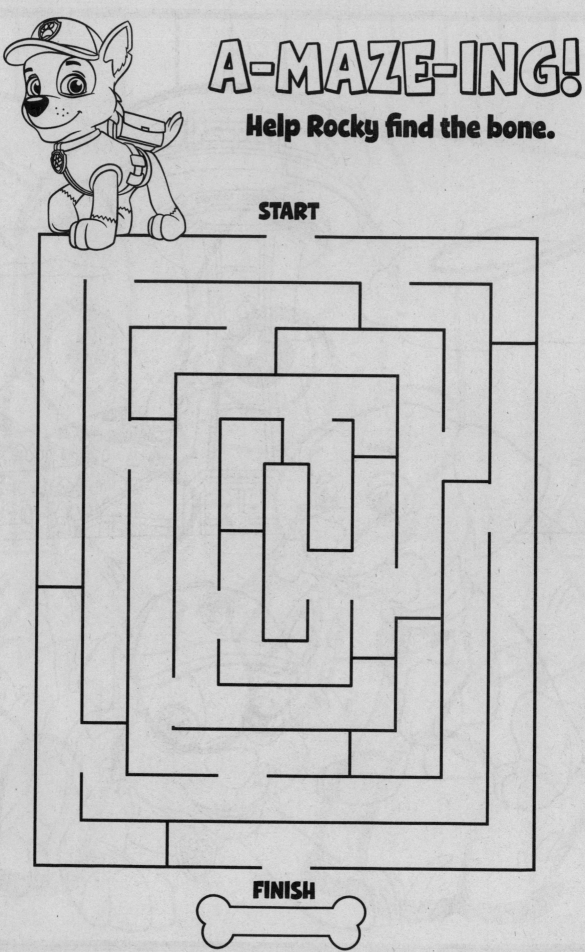

START

FINISH

© 2014 Spin Master. All Rights Reserved.

© 2014 Spin Master. All Rights Reserved.

READY, SET, GET WET!

© 2014 Spin Master. All Rights Reserved.

© 2014 Spin Master. All Rights Reserved.

HOW MANY?

How many tennis balls do you see? Answer: _____

How many bones? Answer: _____

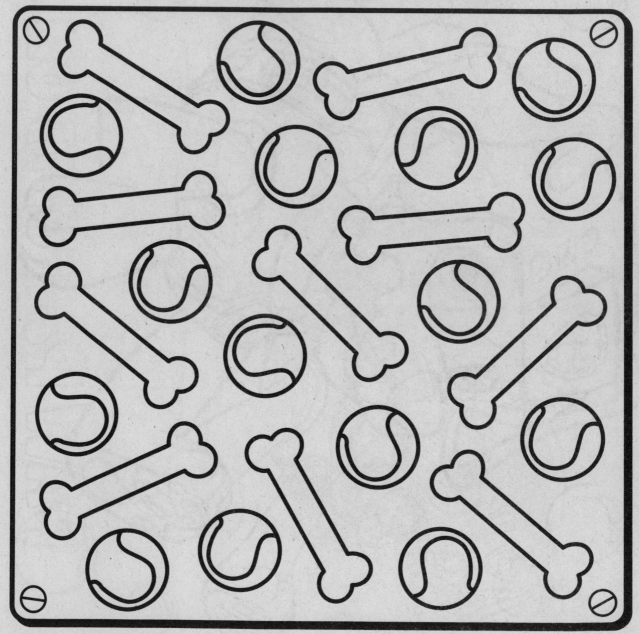

© 2014 Spin Master. All Rights Reserved.

Answer: 15 Tennis Balls, 10 Bones

PAW Patrol is on a roll!

© 2014 Spin Master. All Rights Reserved.

Whenever there's trouble, just yelp for help!

© 2014 Spin Master. All Rights Reserved.